FANTASMUS presents

www.fantasmus.com

Introduction

Once upon a time........really should be the beginning of this book, as the artist - Claus Brusen - is known and respected for his ability to tell fairy tales through his paintings. Over the last nearly 40 years Claus has created a unique and very special world called Nactalius, in which we get to meet all the quircky and nice creatures we normally just dream about. Claus has an ability to make even the weirdest and horrific beings nice and cosy.

This is a visual story of a man that lets us all into his friendly and humours world. Enjoy!

The early years
Surrealism

Only 16 years old Claus Brusen started doing sketches and drawing motives more and more surreal - mainly inspired by Dali. His first real painting in oil was made and that was the beginning of a long and extraordinary carreer as an artist. A period that was experimental and slowly led Claus towards his very own stile as an artist.

The very first sketch

No title · 80 x 50 cm · Oil on canvas

No title · 80 x 50 cm · Oil on canvas

No title · 80 x 50 cm · Oil on canvas

No title · 80 x 50 cm · Oil on canvas

11

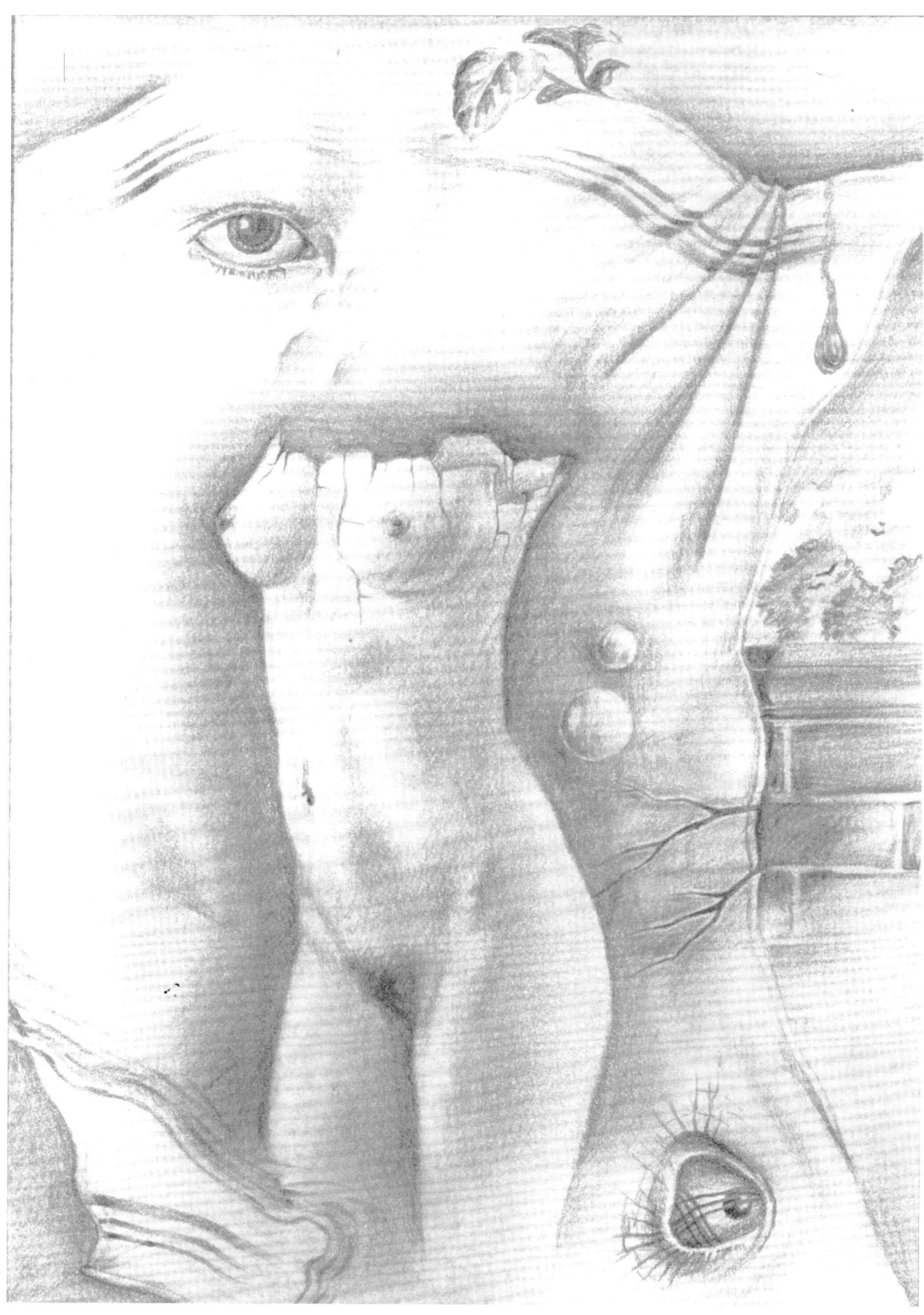

Thoughts of a Towel - 20 x 15 cm - Pencil on Papir

No title · 80 x 50 cm · Oil on canvas

No title · 80 x 50 cm · Oil on canvas

Faces · 28 x 22 cm · Oil on canvas

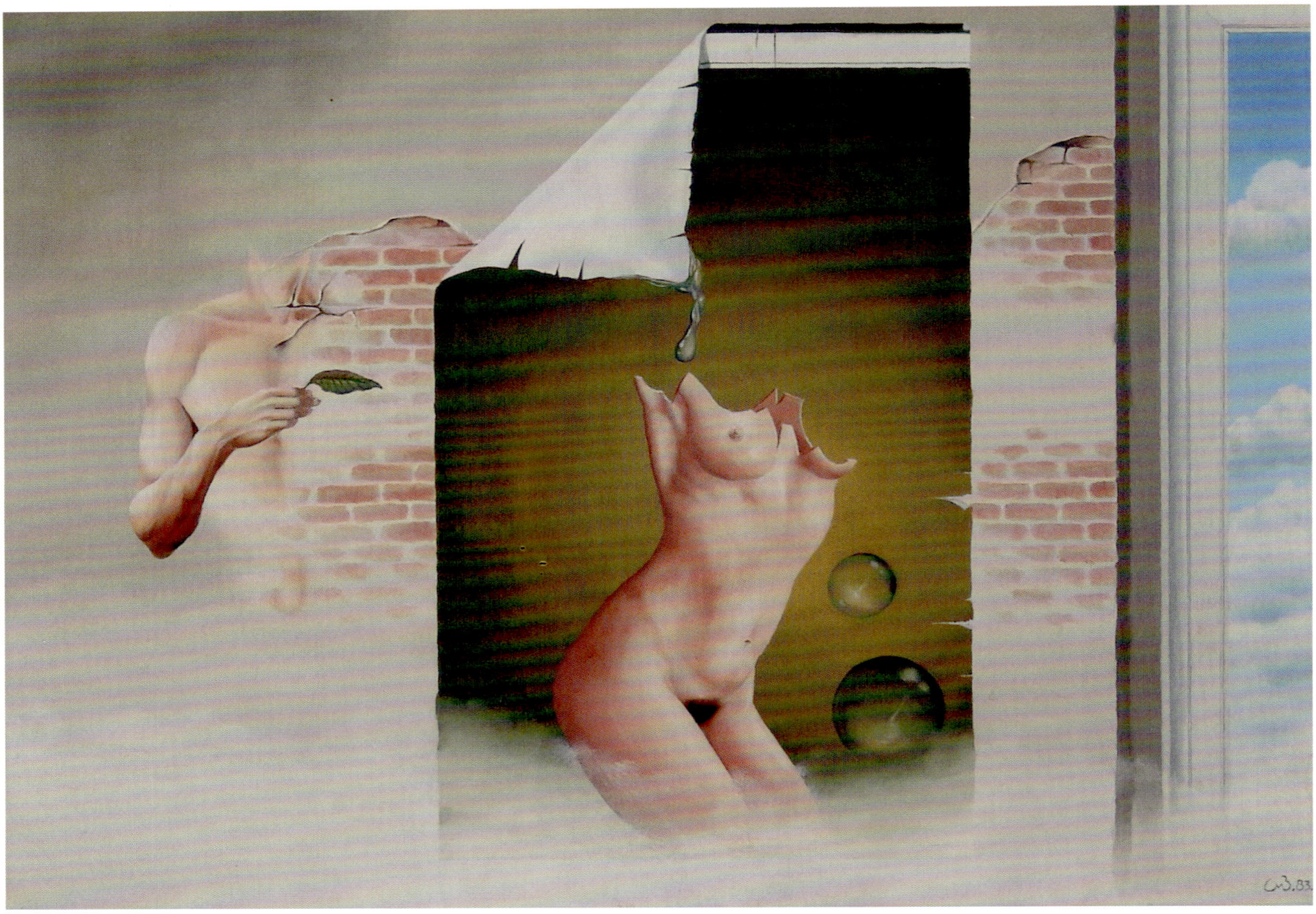

Hold on to your Dreams · 80 x 50 cm · Oil on panel

Hold on to your Dreams · 60 x 40 cm · Oil on panel

Flower Fairies · 30 x 20 cm · Oil on panel

Black Bride · 80 x 120 cm · Oil on canvas

From surreal to fairy tales

In the Forest

The major transfer from painting more or less inspired by the surrealism to creating a whole new world of his own happened practically over night while having a dream i which the name "Nactalius" suddenly came to life. Claus Brusen very own world in which notting bad ever dominates, there's always room for everyone - especially all the quircky creatures and beings with nowhere else to go. Mainly this world is being shown in the deep, cosy forest but also in the pretty blue skye. And sometimes the odd ones from the naughty side want to be part of this

Nactalius (My Dream) · 80 x 50 cm · Oil on linen

Tiny Fairy · 20 x 30 cm · Oil on panel

Fairy Master's Judgement · 50 x 80 cm · Oil on panel

A Gentle Touch of Conversation · 20 x 30 cm · Oil on panel

Sorrow · 30 x 40 cm · Oil on panel

21

Forest Playground · 40 x 60 cm · Oil on panel

Magic Forest III · 40 x 30 cm · Oil on panel

Bad Behaviour · 20 x 30 cm · Oil on panel

The Finding · 80 x 120 cm cm · Oil on panel

25

Old and Wise · 30 x 20 cm · Oil on panel

Nephelia · 30 x 20 cm · Oil on panel

Dreamforest · 80 x 122 cm · Oil on panel

Dragonmaster · 20 x 15 cm · Oil on panel

The Little Prince and his true Guard · 30,1 x 23,6 cm · Oil on panel

Flower Fairy and the Frog Prince · 30 x 45 cm · Oil on panel

Yellow Bird · 75 x 60 cm · Oil on panel

Let the Magic begin · 20 x 15 cm · Oil on panel

Nature gives and we are grateful · 30 x 45 cm · Oil on panel

Protector of Magic · 30 x 20 cm · Oil on panel

My Love · 50 x 40 cm · Oil on panel

My Love · 50 x 40 cm · Sketch

Secret Garden II · 27 x 22 cm · Oil on panel

Sercret Garden - Life of Nature · 40 x 30 cm · Oil on panel

The Flower Fairy Parade · Triptych - 42,5 x 17 - 42,5 x 37 - 42,5 x 17 cm · Oil on panel

The Art Committee · 27 x 22 cm · Oil on panel

Babble Nonsense · 30,1 x 23,6 cm · Oil on panel

Mr. & Mrs. Birdy van Strut · 22,6 x 15,4 cm · Oil on panel

Magic outside the Box · 20 x 30 cm · Oil on panel

Tommelise · 40 x 50 cm · Oil on panel

Tea for Two · 20 x 15 cm · Oil on panel

Strawberry Man · 26 x 23 cm · Oil on panel

Teasing · 40 x 50 cm · Oil on panel

The Happy Strawberry Collectors · 35 x 30 cm · Oil on panel

45

Nactalius · 110 x 170 cm · Oil on panel

The Kiss · 20 x 30 cm · Oil on panel

Audiens · 40 x 50 cm · Oil on panel

Summer and Winter · 27 x 22 cm · Oil on panel

The Proposal · 27 x 22 cm · Oil on panel

An Ordinary Day in Nactalius · 35,5 x 45,5 cm · Oil on panel

Little Magic · Triptych - 42,5 x 17 - 42,5 x 37 - 42,5 x 17 cm · Oil on panel

Time for Tea · 27 x 22 cm · Oil on panel

The Odd Couple I · Ø cm · Oil on panel

The Happy Parade · 80 x 122 cm · Oil on panel

Smalltalk I · 27 x 22 cm · Oil on panel

Smalltalk II · 27 x 22 cm · Oil on panel

The Art Committee · 50 x 60 cm · Oil on panel

The Guardian Owl · 24 x 20 cm · Oil on panel

Sir Owl · 17,8 x 12,6 cm · Oil on panel

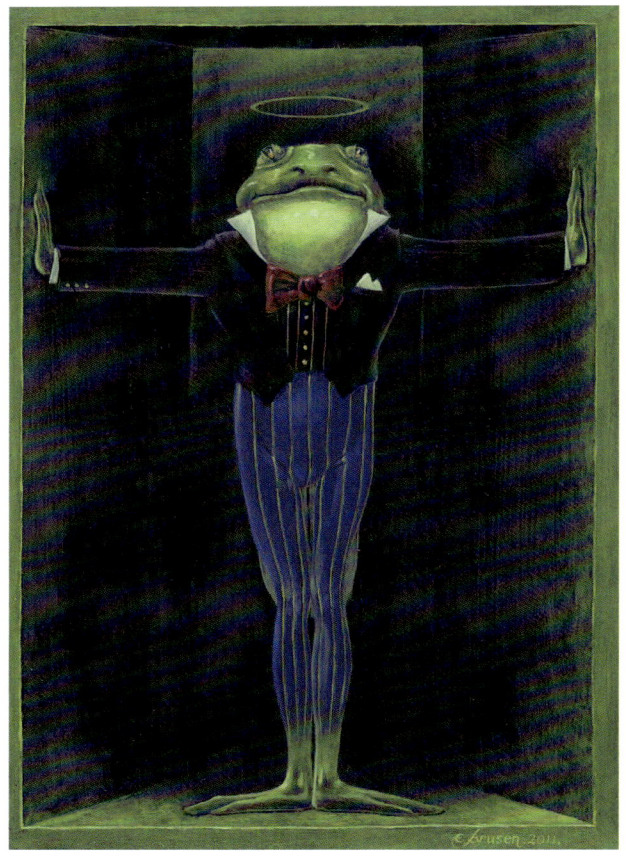

Frog in a Box · 17,8 x 12,6 cm · Oil on panel

Mr. Nice Mouse · 17,8 x 12,6 cm · Oil on panel

The making of "The Battle of Strawberry Lane"

The Battle of Strawberry Lane · 45 x 80 cm · Oil on panel

King Toad's Capture of the Butterfly Virgin · 40 x 30 cm · Oil on panel

�# In the Sky

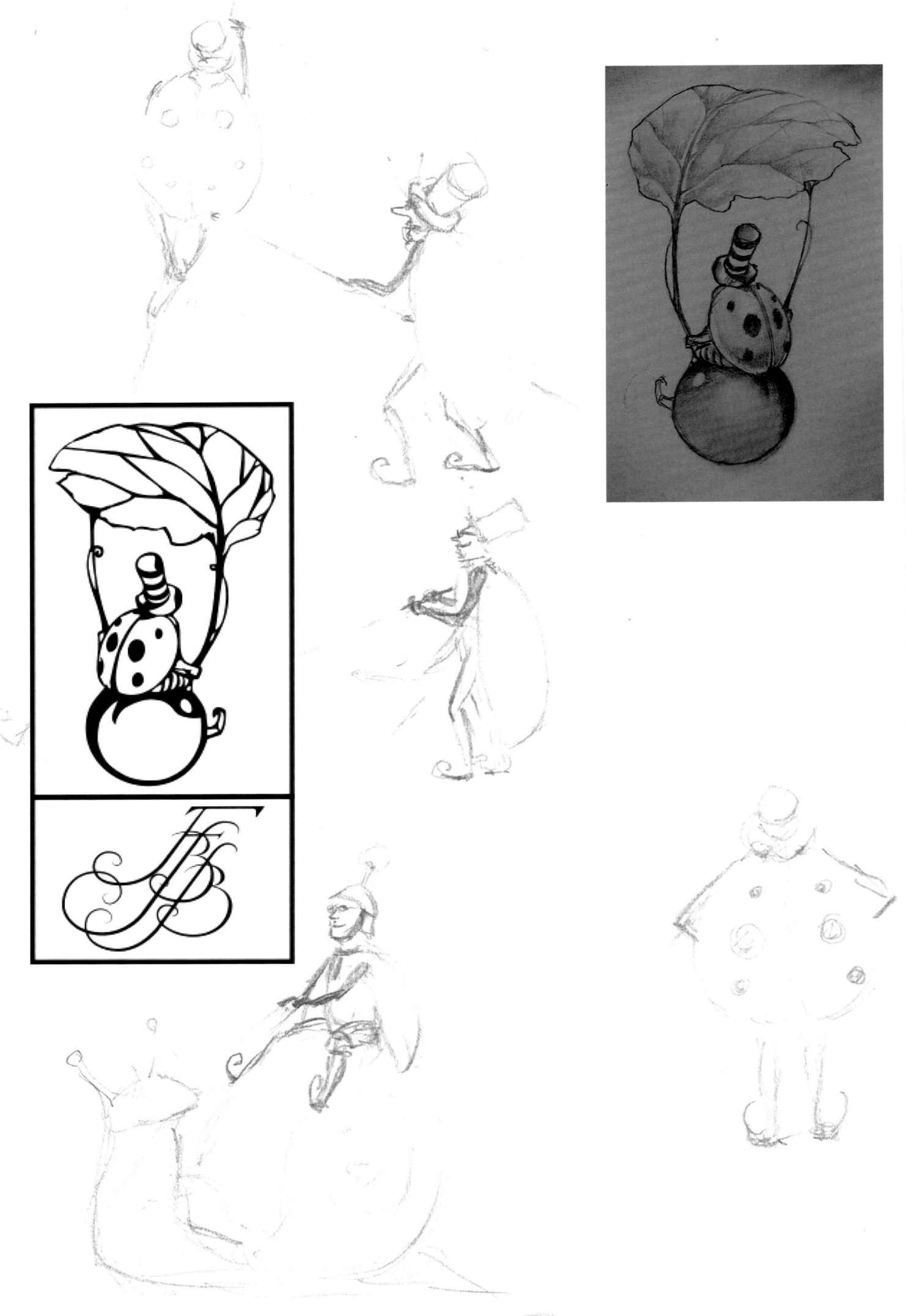

Ladybird · 17,8 x 12,6 cm · Oil on panel

Flowers · 22 x 27 cm · Oil on panel

Moonmadness · 75 x 100 cm · Oil on panel

Friendship · 22 x 27 cm · Oil on panel

The Dragon · 27 x 22 cm · Oil on panel

Flower Fairy · 50 x 40 cm · Oil on panel

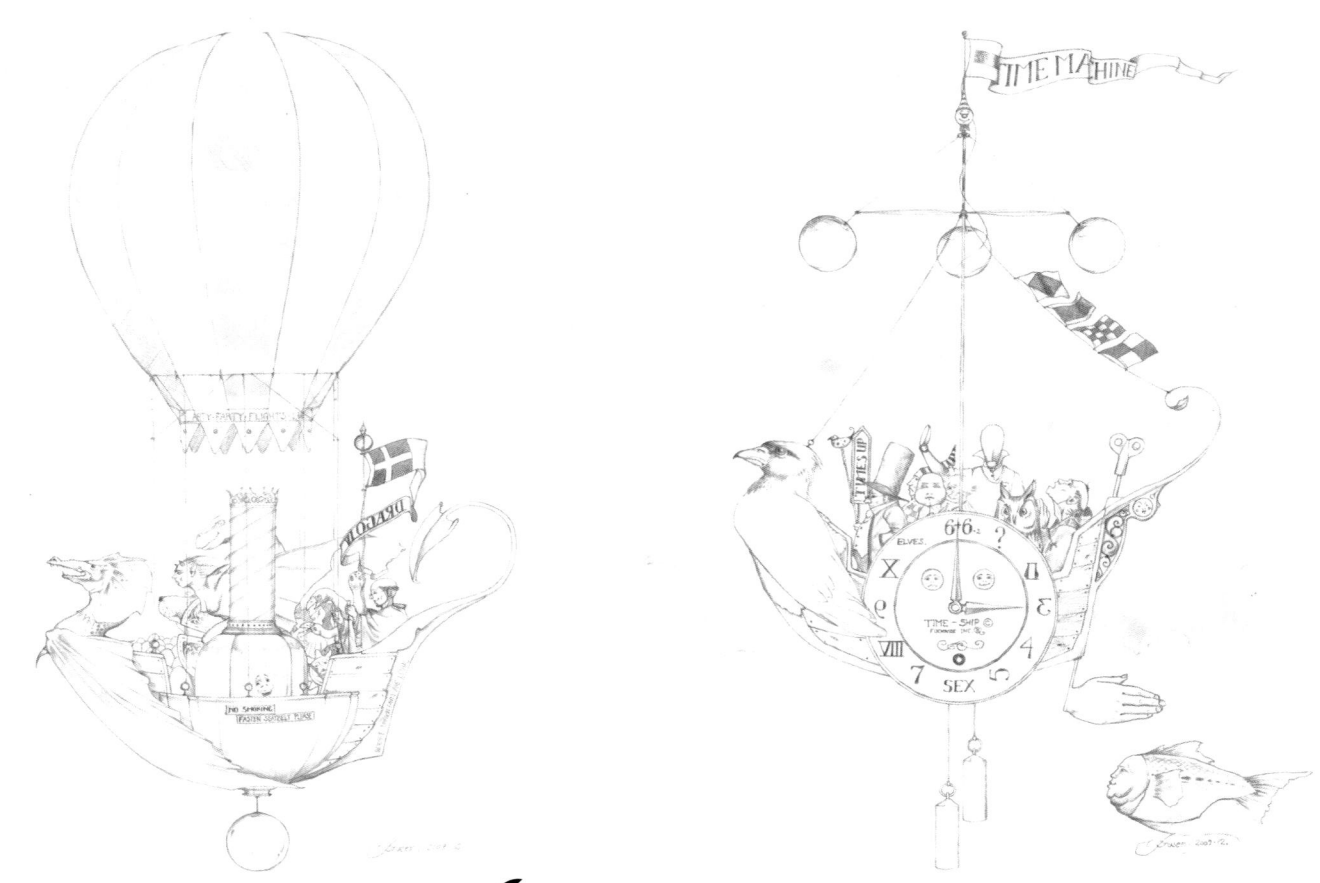

Sky Boats

Ship of Fools · 70 x 50 cm · Oil on panel

Flying towards Nactalius · 60 x 80 cm · Oil on panel

Ode to Roger Dean · 29,7 x 42 cm · Oil on panel

The Excursion · Triptych - 42,5 x 17 - 42,5 x 37 - 42,5 x 17 cm · Oil on panel

The Question · 40 x 30 cm · Oil on panel

Musical forest

Pinneappelis Musicanta · 27 x 22 cm · Oil on panel

Campanula Concerto · 22 x 27 cm · Oil on panel

The Duet · 22 x 27 cm · Oil on panel

Cello Concerto in D Minor · 50 x 60 cm · Oil on panel

Trees in Nactalius

Old Sad Oak · 60 x 40 cm · Oil on panel

Old Forest I · 18 x 14 cm · Oil on panel

Old Forest IV · 18 x 14 cm · Oil on panel

Old Tree XII · 17,8 x 12,6 cm · Oil on panel

Old Tree X · 17,8 x 12,6 cm · Oil on panel

Pin Up Flower Fairy · 40 x 30 cm · Oil on panel

The naughty side

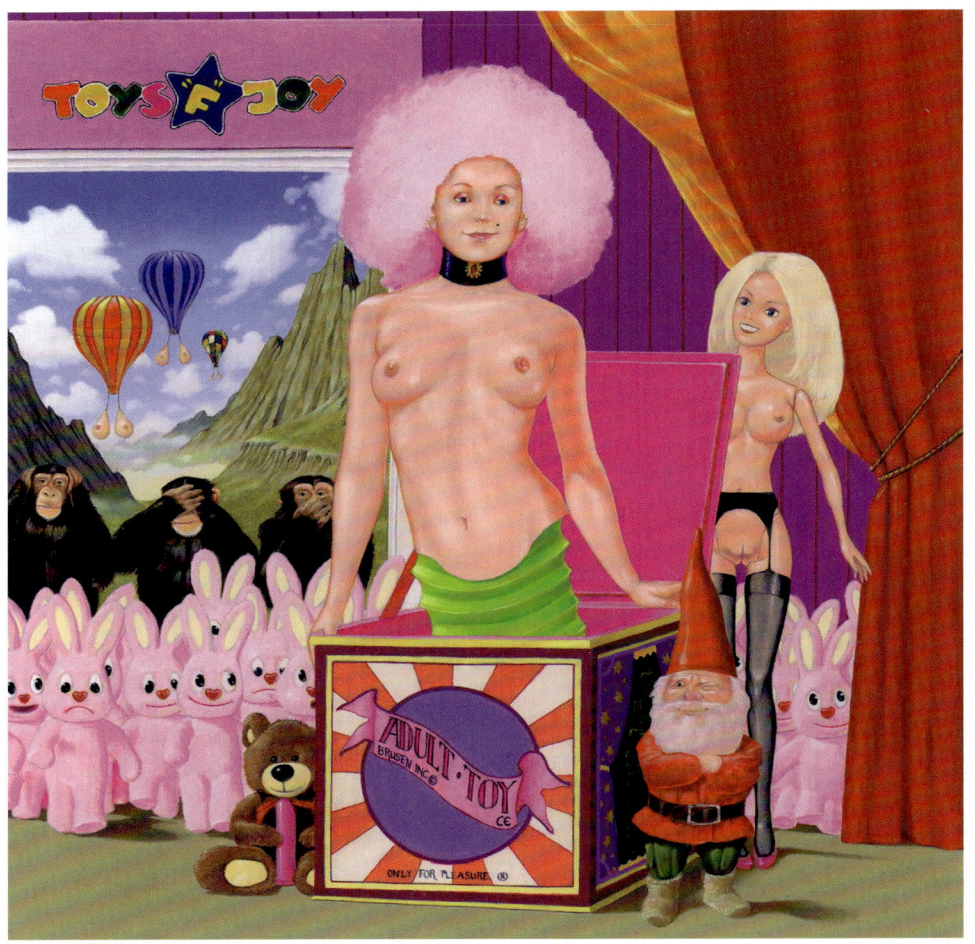
Toy Story II · 30 x 30 cm · Oil on panel

Toy Story III · 30 x 30 cm · Oil on panel

Toy Story I - The Good, The Bad and The Ugly · 27 x 22 cm · Oil on panel

Sketch for Eruption

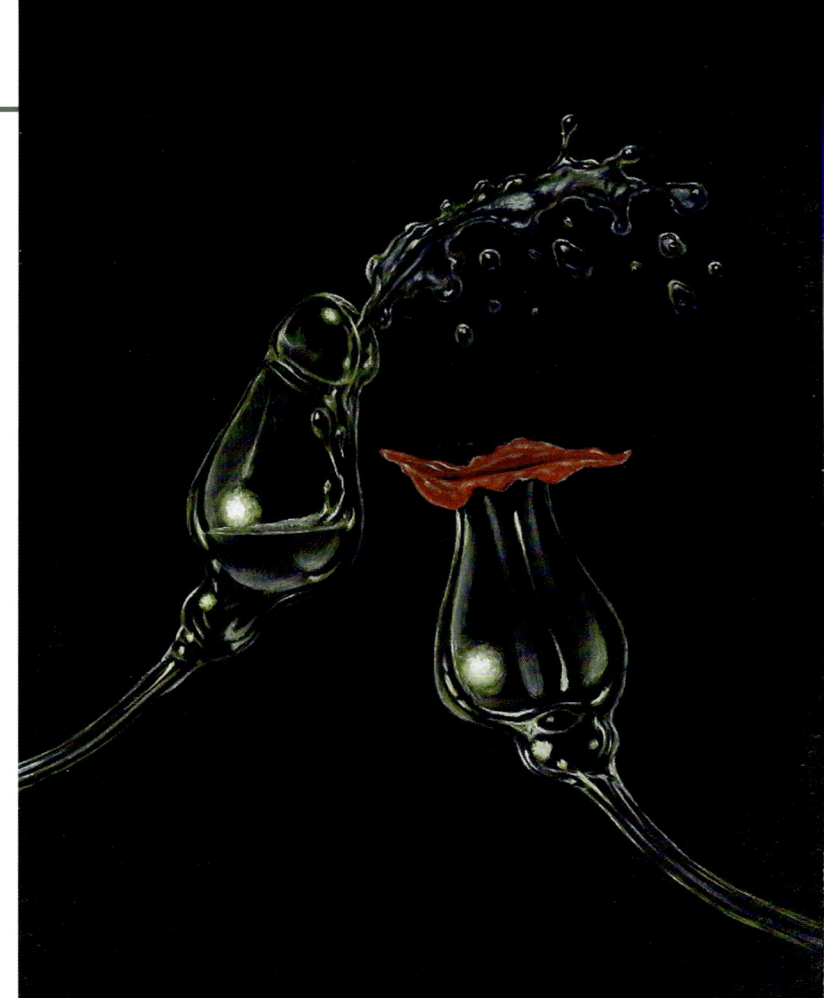

Fountains of Life · 17,8 x 12,6 cm · Oil on panel

Eruption · 40 x 30 cm · Oil on panel

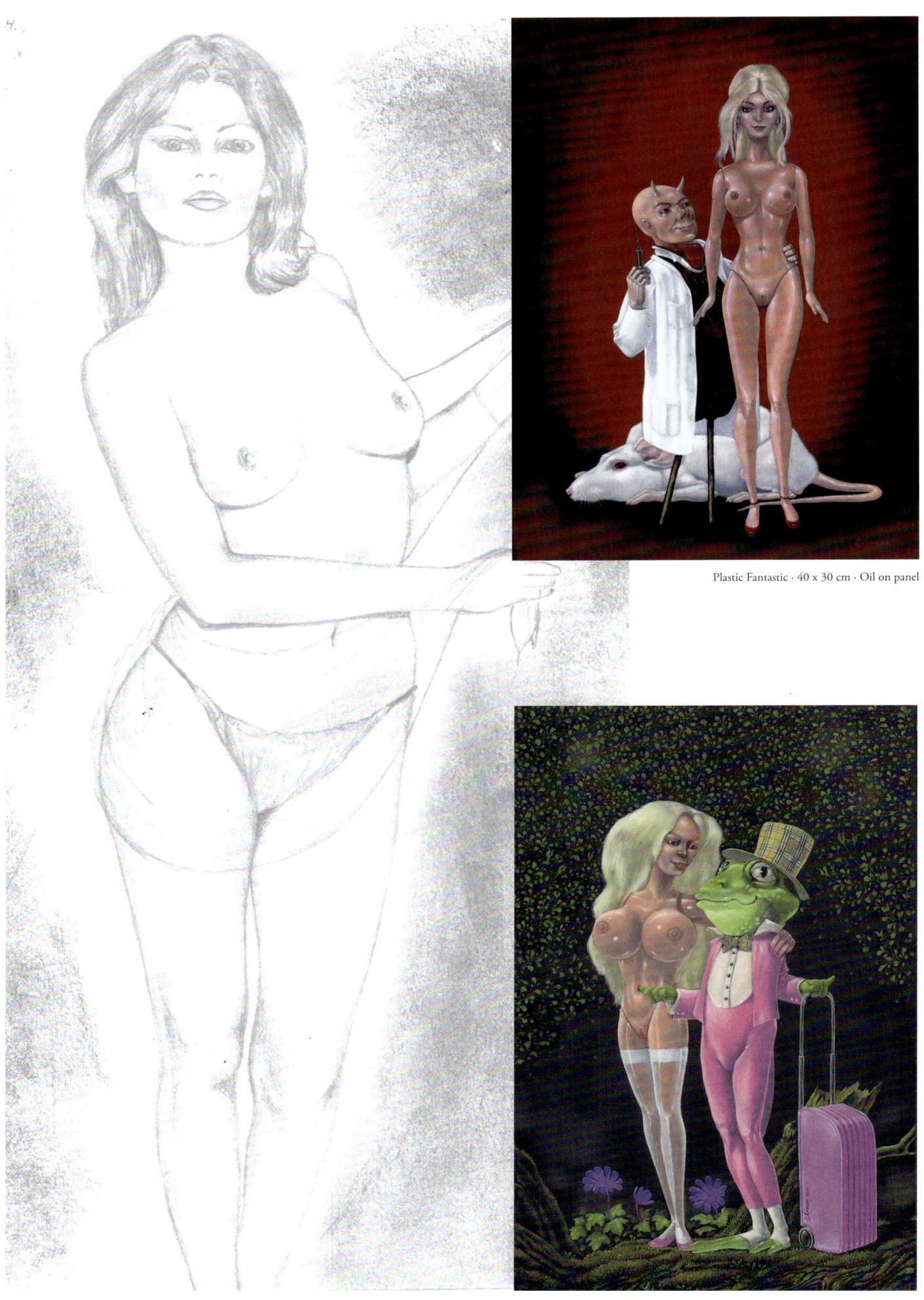

Pecil Drawing/Sketch · Pin Up Girl

Plastic Fantastic · 40 x 30 cm · Oil on panel

The Odd Couple III · 30,5 x 22,8 cm · Oil on panel

Pin Up Venus of Nactalius · 40 x 45 cm · Oil on panel

Venus of Nactalius · 34 x 45 cm · Oil on panel

Beatrice · Triptych - 42,5 x 17 - 42,5 x 37 - 42,5 x 17 cm · Oil on panel

Sketch for Beatrice

Beatrice and Dante - closed · Triptych - 42,5 x 17 - 42,5 x 37 - 42,5 x 17 cm · Oil on panel

Portraits
&
Commissions

Sannie · Drawing/pencil on paper

Sannie · Drawing/pencil on paper

Jo and Steve Hackett, Claus Brusen and Mette Bisgaard

Numero Uno · 40 x 30 cm · Pencil on paper

"Rebirth" - Jo and Steve Hackett · 27 x 22 cm · Oil on panel

Mr. and Mrs. Nannestad · 40 x 50 cm · Oil on panel

Alice Makes Wonderland · 40 x 30 cm · Pencil on paper

Wordenskjold · 45 x 17 cm · Oil on Copper

Mr. Julius Arnfeldt · 50 x 40 cm · Oil on panel

HRH Prince Henrik ordering 2 paintings, Mrs. Struggle and a Walrus

Claus Brusen, Tegner Bruno and Mette Bisgaard

I am the Walrus · 17,8 x 12,6 cm · Oil on panel

Mr. Struggle · 17,8 x 12,6 cm · Oil on panel

Tegner Bruno · 40 x 50 cm · Oil on panel

Exhitions and projects

Throughout the years Claus Brusen have been participating in various exhibtions both i Denmark and many other countries. Furthermore Claus has been a pioneer for the genre Magic Realisme worldwide. As both a curator and a publisher of art book this has led to many interesting experiences and a lot of friendships and meetings with both painters and musicians worldwide. It goes without saying that Claus is wide respected for his efforts. Claus has had the pleasure of working with some of his own personal idols and also befrieding some of them. Combining art with music have been a new way of presenting both genres and his aim to establish a museum for fantastic art in Denmark is also one of the wishes for the future.

Some of the meeting worth mentioning are with the late Patrick James Woodroffe. Claus' absolute number 1 idol. One of the genres geniouses. He also became a very good friend over the years. Claus have had the pleasuer of having sold many a painting to His Royal Highness Prince consort Henrik and in now in the process of portraing him in Nactalius. Record cover artist Mark Wilkinson and his wife Julie have been great supporters as have musicians such as Fish, Steve Hackett and Anthony Phillips.

Claus enjoying a peacefull moment with Patrick James Woodroffe

 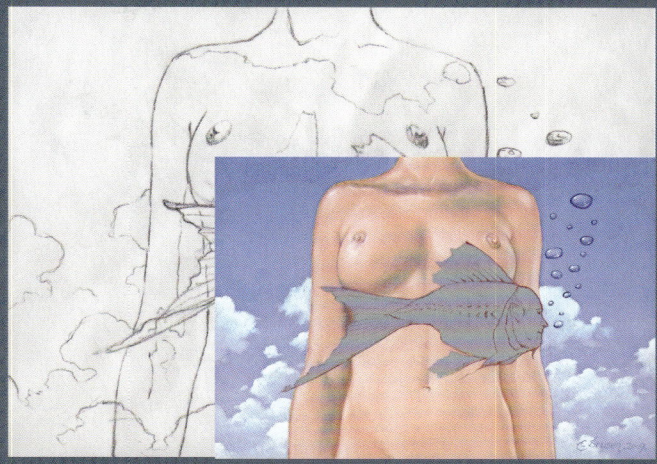

The Dante Exhibition in Denmark:
Monica Fagan, Claus Brusen, Mark Wilkinson, Fish, Katie Webb and Morten Eliassen

Claus' painting for Fish

The Dante Exhibition in Denmark: José Roosevelt, Danny Evo Heinricht, Paul Erland, Michael Hiep, Richard Pernsteiner, Mark Wilkinson, Peter van Oostzanen, Patrick James Woodroffe, Siegfried Zademack, Claus Brusen, Annabella Claudia, Monica Fagan, Reinhard Schmidt, Anne-Fieke Later, Elisabeth de Lunde, Eugené Later

Claus Brusen in Vienna with Mr. Ernst Fuchs

At Phantasten Museum in Vienna: Kate Eggleston-Wirtz, Eike Ertzmoniet, Claus Brusen, Brigid Marlin, Michel de San Ouen, Mr. Ernst Fuchs, Erich Peichl and Professor Gerhard Habarta

Claus Brusen in Paris

Anthony Phillips

Robert and Trine - Claus' children - Patrick James Woodroffe and Claus

HRH Prince Henrik at a visit in FANTASMUS

Mette and Claus in FANTASMUS

Kemal Ramujkic, Claus Brusen, Zeljko Durovic

Claus at the Grand Prix in Sicily

Claus Brusen and Ambassadeur Valentin Poriazov in front of Nactalius in FANTASMUS

Steven Kenny, Dannie Evo Heinricht and Claus Brusen

The Miniatures

To raise money for this book project Claus decided to paint some miniatures to sell for a very reasonable price. It has been intended al along just to raise the exact amount of money to cover cost. 25 miniatures was made and put up for sale. Before knowing what Claus had painted buyers could pay and thereby get a number accordingly to which they could choose paintings at the end of the project. Along with the painting the buyers will receive a copy of this book and a fine arts print of the cover of the book.

A very special thank you to the following persons who made my wish and this book come true:

Hans Jørn Hansen, #25 To be or not to be.... a Ladybug
Hanne Josefsen, #2 Flowers
Inger Marie Bisgaard, #Wise Old Owl
Hans Olof Olsson, #20 Freaky Thing
Anni Rasmussen, #4 Mushroom - The Family
Peter Holger Eriksen, #22 Fishermans Delight
Geert Petersen, #1 Asking for Guidance & #18 Strange Flower
Tove Bak, #6 Froggy the Wanderer
Michael Hiep, #Roots
Tegner Bruno, #3 Bottom Button Inc.
Jan Christensen, #15 Early Springs
Frida Franko-Dossar og Martin Hedegaard, #14 Seeds of Life
Nikolai og Dorota, #7 The Little Trumpeteer
Birthe Kjærgaard, #17 Ready to Fly
Mikkel Knudsen, #16 Ye Old Tree
Finn Thomsen, # Peter the Tiny Dragon

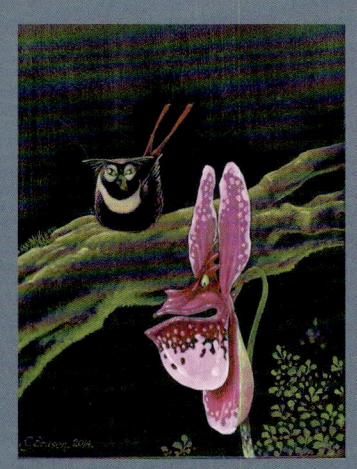

Resume

Claus Brusen

1960	Born in Aalborg, DK
1977	Started drawing more intens inspired by Dali among others.
1983	Had my first exhibition at an Art Museum, with drawings and sketches.
1998	Became serious and started to work as a proffessionel artist
2004	Had my first exhibition abroad, at Interart Gallery NY, USA
2005	My first solo exhibition at a official Art Museum, SNYK, Skive Art Museum, DK

From then on I have participated in exhibition in Denmark and around the world, in countries like England, France, The Netherlands, Belgium, Italy "Sicily", Sweden, USA, Austria, among others.

Member of AOI, Society for Art of Imagination

Founder of FANTASMUS. C.A.I.I.R Center for Art of Imaginary International Realism

Was awarded the "Premier Cru Superieur Prize" in the 2008 Annual Society Exhibition at The Brick Lane Gallery, London by Society for Art of Imagination.

September 2009, Castroreale, Sicily. Sinafia, III Grand Prix Internazionale "Italia" recieved 3rd place "Bronze medal".

My paintings can be found in many collections around the world, among these to mention a few:

Commissioned by Saebygaard Trust to do a portrait of the last owner of Saebygaard Manor House. Has sold several works to HRH Prince Henri of Denmark and is currently doing a personal portrait for him.

I have had the pleasure of meeting a lot of my heros and with some of them become very good friends, like Patrick Woodroffe (R.I.P) who is probably my biggest inspiration, and countless more.

www.clausbrusen.com
info@clausbrusen.com

Publications where my work appear.

Monography

Portfolie 2000 - 2003 "Nactalius, a Friendly World by Claus Brusen" SC 28 pages full colour 2004 Edition Brusen
The Fantastic World of Claus Brusen. HC 120 pages full colour 2005. Edition Brusen
"Velkommen til Nactalius" SC 28 pages full colour 2005. Skive Art Museum
Fantasmus presents "The Art of Claus Brusen" HC 136 pages full colour 2014. Edition Brusen - Fantasmus Art Books

Books and Catalogues my work appear in:

H, C. Anderson+ catalogue. SC 60 pages full colour 2005. Edition Brusen
Skive Kunstmuseum, Fantastiske Figurationer - Påskeudstilling 2005. SC 24 pages full colour 2005. Skive Artmuseum
Spectrum 12. "The Best in Contemporary Fantastic Art" HC & SC 208 Pages full colour 2005. Fenner & Fenner - Underwood Books
Galerie Brusen "exhibition catalogue" SC 44 pages full colour 2006. Edition Brusen
Galerie Honingen "Meesterlijke Miniaturen II" "exhibition catalogue" SC 12 pages full colour 2006. Galerie Honingen
Dreamscape 1. "The Best of Imaginary Realism" HC 128 pages full colour 2006. Salbru Publish
Galerie Brusen "exhibition catalogue" SC 16 pages full colour 2007. Edition Brusen
Venus & The Female Intuition "exhibition catalogue" SC 96 pages full colour 2007. Salbru Publish
Dreamscape 2. "The Best of Imaginary Realism" HC 144 pages full colour 2007. Salbru Publish
IMAGINAIRE I. "Magic Realism" HC 148 pages full colour 2008. Edition Brusen - Fantasmus Art Books
Dante, The Divine Comedy. "exhibition catalogue" SC 96 pages full colour 2009. Edition Brusen - Fantasmus Art Books
Grand Prix Internazionale "Italia" Castroreale- Messina "calalogue" SC 76 pages full colour 2009 Safina
101 Kunstnere - 2009. HC 208 pages full colour 2009. JA Aps
IMAGINAIRE II. "Magic Realism" HC 176 pages full colour 2009. Edition Brusen - Fantasmus Art Books
Lexikon der phantastichen Künstler. HC 464 pages 2009. I.F.A.A.
Quadrant Fantasy. "exhibition catalogue" SC 96 pages full colour 2010. Edition Brusen - Fantasmus Art Books
Culture Seeds "catalogue" SC 26 pages full colour 2010. COSM
IMAGINAIRE III. "Magic Realism" HC 200 pages full colour 2010. Edition Brusen - Fantasmus Art Books
Phantasten Museum Wien "Catalogue 2011" HC 312 pages full colour 2011. I.F.A.A
Magical Dreams 2011 "exhibition catalogue" SC 56 pages full colour 2011. Beskidzka Galeria Sztuki
IMAGINAIRE IV. "Magic Realism" HC 168 pages full colour 2011. Edition Brusen - Fantasmus Art Books
Society for Art of Imagination "catalogue" HC 72 pages full colour 2012. I.F.A.A
IMAGINAIRE V. "Magic Realism" HC 112 pages full colour 2013. Edition Brusen - Fantasmus Art Books
IMAGINAIRE VI. "Magic Realism" HC 112 pages full colour 2013. Edition Brusen - Fantasmus Art Books
"Of Beauties and Beasts" "exhibition catalogue" SC full colour 2014. Clement Art gallery
IMAGINAIRE VII. "Magic Realism" HC 176 pages full colour 2014. Edition Brusen - Fantasmus Art Books

My work "Ladybird flying to the land of Make-believe" was used for the cover of a novel called Ladybird Fly, written by Tessa Lorant Warburg. Published by The Thorn Press 2011.

Important exhibitions, as a curator:

2005.
Voergaard Castle, DK, May 2005. H. C. Andersen+ W/ Patrick Woodroffe, UK as the guest of honour.
2006.
In spring 2006 I opened Galerie Brusen in Sæby only with group exhibition with artists from around the world.
2007.
Together with Marcel Salome of Re-Art in The Netherlands, we made Venus & the Female Intuition, a group show featuring Michael Parkes, USA as our guest of honour, at Saebygaard Castle, DK.
This exhibition travelled to Grooningen in The Netherlands ans Nice in France same year over the summer.
2008.
In spring 2008 Galerie Brusen became FANTASMUS and was now more a platform for the fantastic art, curating, publishing and marketing the genre under this new name.
In summer 2008, I curated an exhibition for AOI, Society for Art of Imagination, this was coordinated with Brigid Marlin, UK and Michel de Saint Ouen, UK.
2009.
In summer 2009, I held the third large group show with catalogue, "Dante, The Divine Comedy" with danish artist Carsten Svennson as guest of honour.
This exhibition also travelled to Viechtach, Germany in cooperation with Tourist Bureau of Viechtach.
2010.
Spring 2010 I made Quadrant Fantasy, again a group exhibition with artists from around the world, this was made in collaboration with Strychnin Gallery, Berlin.
Fall 2010 we held the first IMAGINAIRE exhibition, celebrating IMAGINAIRE III. at Hillerod library, north of Copenhagen.
FANTASMUS moved to Copenhagen to continue its endevours in the world of magic art.
2011.
January 2011, I arranged a solo exhibition for Carsten Svennson at FANTASMUS in Copenhagen.
June 2011, I curated a Memorial exhibition at SNYK, Skive Art Museum for Carsten Svennson who died in the early spring same year. This was called Carsten Svennson and friends, and was build up around artists Carsten have meet during his travels around the world with his art.
2012.
From 2012 All curating became together with Mette with whom I meet in spring 2011.
Our first curating job together was in April, called "Freakshow" this was held again at Hillerod library. A groupshow in the line that had started in 2005 with H. C. Andersen+
2014.
November 2014 we Mette and I, the first major IMAGINAIRE exhibition, presenting artist on a larger scale who are in our books, this was for book no. 7.

Beside these large scale events, I have held many smaller exhibition for artists and from 2011 when we became a pair, we had even more smaller events as Mette took over a large part of this job.

FANTASMUS PRESENTS
The Art of Claus Brusen

First published in Denmark 2015
Copyright © 2015 - FBB-FANTASMUS Bisgaard Brusen - FANTASMUS Artbooks

First edition

All rights reserved to the publisher. No part of this book may be reproduced or transmitted in any form, mannor or media including photography, recording or any other information storage and retrieval system, nor may pages be applied to any material, cut, trimmed or sized to alter the excisting trim sizes (or) matted or framed with the intent to create other products for sale or resale or profit in any manor whatsoever, withour prior permission in writing from the publisher and/or the artists.

The Art of Claus Brusen
2015, with reg.
ISBN: 978-993936-7-1
EAN: 97899393671

All text by Mette Torp Bisgaard
Set in Adobe Garamond Pro and Apple Chancery
Design and Layout by Mette Torp Bisgaard, FANTASMUS

Cover: Smalltalk II, Oil on panel

www.fantasmus.com

INDEX

Page 2 - Introduction
Page 4 - The Early Years - Surrealism
Page 16 - From surreal to fairy tales - In the forest
Page 66 - In the Sky
Page 78 - Musical Forest
Page 84 - Trees in Nactalius
Page 90 - The Naughty Side
Page 102 - Portraits and Commissions
Page 114 - Exhibitions and Projects
Page 120 - The Miniatures
Page 122 - Resume

FANTASMUS ARTBOOKS PRESENTS
THE IMAGINAIRE SERIES

IMAGINAIRE VIII
Release date October 2015
Guest of honour: Michael Maschka - Germany

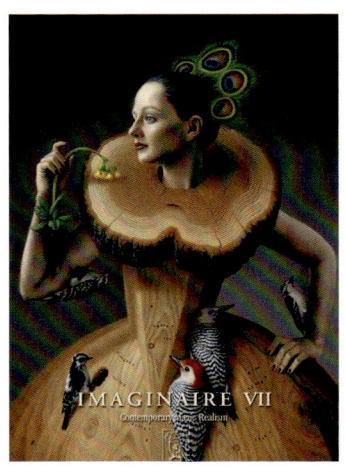

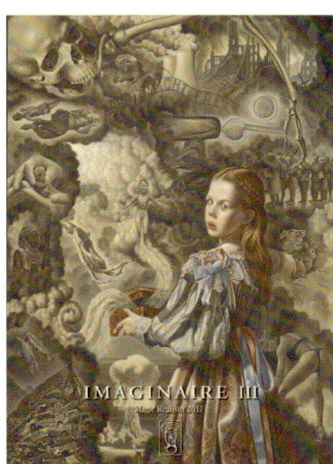
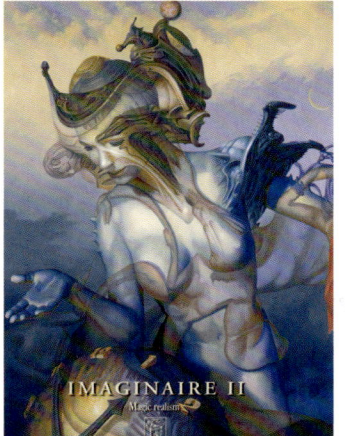

Check at www.fantasmus.com for this and many more books and events!